Overclocking Reality

A Radical Exploration of Perception and Sensory Processes

Freudian Trips

Copyright Page

Disclaimer

The views and opinions expressed in this book are those of the author(s) and do not necessarily reflect the official policy or position of any other agency, organization, employer, or company. The contents of this book are for informational and educational purposes only and are not intended to serve as professional advice, diagnosis, or treatment.

The information provided in this book is believed to be accurate and reliable as of the date of publication. However, it may include some errors or inaccuracies, and no warranty or guarantee is provided regarding the accuracy, timeliness, or applicability of the content.

Readers are encouraged to consult with professional philosophers, educators, or other qualified professionals where appropriate for personalized advice. The author(s) and publisher shall not be liable for any loss, damage, or harm caused or alleged to be caused, directly or indirectly, by the information or ideas contained, suggested, or referenced in this book.

By reading this book, the reader acknowledges and agrees that they are solely responsible for how they interpret and apply the information contained herein.

This book may also include references to other works, studies, and sources. These references are provided for further reading and exploration and do not imply endorsement or validation of the specific theories, viewpoints, or interpretations presented in those works.

Introduction - Unraveling the Veil

Have you ever walked on a beach, feeling the cool waves brushing against your toes, or savored the first sip of your morning coffee, letting its aroma and warmth envelop you? These are the wonders of perception – an ongoing, vivid movie where you are both the main character and the audience.

Let's dive deep into this magic, shall we?

The Magic Behind What We Feel and See

Perception is like the colorful brush strokes on a canvas. It's the way our brain paints the world around us based on the information our senses send its way. Close your eyes for a moment and imagine a world without it. A void. A blank canvas. Pretty unthinkable, right?

From the simplest things, like the gentle feel of a soft blanket, to the more complex, like recognizing the face of a loved one from afar, it's perception that's at work, allowing us to experience and navigate our world.

But Why Does This Matter?

It's not just about seeing or feeling things. Our perceptions shape our reality. Have you ever noticed how two people can experience the same event and yet recount it differently? That's because each person's perception is their own unique window to the world, influenced by their past experiences, beliefs, and even moods.

Remember when you believed in fairy tales or were scared of the imaginary monsters under your bed? Our perceptions then were vastly different from now. And as we grow, they continue to evolve, proving that the reality we live in is continuously shaped and reshaped by how we perceive it.

Our Journey Ahead

In "Overclocking Reality", we're about to embark on a thrilling journey. We'll discover how our basic senses, like sight and touch, lay the foundation of our perceptions. We'll learn about the marvel that is our brain – the grand orchestrator of all our experiences. We'll explore the mysterious realms where our perceptions get a little fuzzy, or where they might even play tricks on us!

But we're not stopping there. We'll go beyond the everyday and peer into extraordinary perceptions, like those of people who can "see" sounds or "taste" colors. And finally, we'll gaze into the future, where the lines between our natural perception and technology-aided perception blur.

By the end of this journey, you'll not only understand the wonders of perception but also appreciate the magnificent world it crafts around us each day. So, let's buckle up and set out on this enlightening adventure, breaking through the veil that often shrouds the magic of perception.

Ready? Let's turn the page and dive in!

Chapter 1: The Senses - The Gateways to Perception

Imagine you're a detective, and the world is an ongoing mystery. How would you solve the case? You'd need clues, right? Well, in the captivating enigma of life, our five senses are the vital clues that allow us to interpret, understand, and truly immerse ourselves in the story of our existence. Let's meet these extraordinary detectives of perception!

1. Sight: Our Personal Movie Projector

Ever noticed how a rainbow can brighten up even the gloomiest days or how the sight of your favorite dish makes your mouth water? That's the magic of sight, the ability of our eyes to catch light and colors and turn them into vivid imagery in our minds. Our eyes are like cameras, constantly capturing the world around us and playing it back in the theater of our brain.

2. Hearing: The Symphony of Sound

Close your eyes for a moment. Even without seeing, you can still hear the hum of the world around you - the chirping of birds, the distant chatter, or the rhythmic beating of your own heart. Our ears pick up vibrations in the air and translate them into the sounds we recognize. From a baby's laughter to our favorite songs, hearing adds layers of depth to our perception.

3. Touch: Feeling the World's Embrace

Remember the warmth of a hug or the tickle of grass under your bare feet? Through touch, we feel the world and its textures. Our skin is this incredible sensor pad, filled with nerve endings that send signals to our brain every time we touch or are touched. Whether it's the chill of an ice cube or the softness of a kitten's fur, touch connects us directly to our surroundings.

4. Taste: The Spice of Life

The zesty tang of a lemon, the sweet delight of chocolate, or the comforting taste of your mom's homemade soup – it's all thanks to our taste buds. Our tongue is like a flavor scanner. With every bite and sip, it explores the different flavors, making meals not just a necessity, but a celebration.

5. Smell: Memory's Time Machine

Ever caught a whiff of something and found yourself transported back in time? Maybe to your childhood or a memorable holiday? That's the power of smell. Our nose detects thousands of scents, and each can evoke powerful emotions and memories. A simple aroma can make us feel safe, nostalgic, or even adventurous.

The Grand Picture

With these five senses combined, we piece together our reality. They're our gateways, our bridges, our interpreters. When you watch a sunset, it's not just the sight but the gentle breeze you feel (touch), the distant sound of waves (hearing), the salty taste in the air (taste), and the scent of the evening flowers (smell) that make the experience complete.

In essence, our senses are like five different instruments in an orchestra, each playing its unique tune. When they come together, they create the symphony of our perception, allowing us to dance through the vibrant tapestry of life.

Stay tuned, because as we venture further, we'll discover the incredible ways our senses and brain work hand in hand to paint the world in the colors of our perception. Onwards to the next chapter of our enlightening journey!

Chapter 2: The Brain - The Grand Orchestrator

Imagine the brain as the grand maestro in the concert hall of your consciousness. Just as the conductor transforms the organized chaos of instruments into a symphony, your brain weaves together the inputs from your senses into the coherent experience that is your reality.

Let's peek behind the scenes to see how the brain works its magic, shall we?

Making Sense of the Sensory Soundtrack

Your senses are constantly buzzing, humming, flashing messages to your brain like a busy orchestra. Light hits your eyes. Soundwaves vibrate in your ears. Your skin tingles from touch. How does your brain take this chaotic sensory soundtrack and transform it into something you can understand?

Your Brain's Secret Sauce - Patterns and Connections

Here's the secret. Your brain thrives on finding patterns. Whenever information from your senses reaches your inner maestro, it looks for ways to organize it into patterns it recognizes. It matches these patterns to memories and past experiences already stored within its convoluted folds.

Based on these patterns, your brain begins making connections, linking related sensory details together. A flash of white here, the smell of antiseptic there. These clues converge to create an understanding of your environment. It's how your perceptions take form!

Your brain may seem like a mystery, but its methods reveal an elegance. Out of sensorial chaos, it builds a harmonic picture of the world unique to you. Understanding this interplay of sensory patterns and connections brings us one step closer to unraveling the grand orchestrator within us all.

Let's continue following the melody in the next chapter, yes? Onwards!

Chapter 3: The Mind-Body Puzzle: Understanding Ourselves a Bit Deeper

Let's take a moment to ponder a fun question: Are we merely made up of cells, blood, and bones, or is there something more to us, something unseen? Like the magical essence that makes a puppet dance, what animates us? This question has been at the heart of one of the greatest debates of all time - the tussle between two ideas: physicalism and dualism.

Physicalism: We Are What We Are Made Of

Imagine building a robot. Once you've attached all its wires, given it a battery, and programmed its software, it moves and interacts, seemingly coming to life. Similarly, physicalism argues that we are like incredibly sophisticated machines. All our emotions, thoughts, and perceptions arise from the intricate workings of our body, especially our brain. So, when we feel happy, scared, or curious, it's because of the various chemicals and electric signals in our brain. There's no need for an additional magical essence; our bodies and their processes are enough to explain everything about us.

Dualism: Two Sides of the Coin

Now, imagine that robot again. No matter how advanced it becomes, can it truly feel love or ponder its own existence? Dualism says there's more to us than just the physical. According to this view, we have two essential parts: our material body and an immaterial mind or soul. It's like a beautiful dance duo where the body is the dancer you can see, while the mind or soul is the music guiding its every move. Our feelings, consciousness, and perceptions are because of this soul or mind dancing in harmony with our body.

Why Does This Debate Matter?

You might be wondering, "Okay, these are fascinating ideas, but why should I care?" Well, this debate shapes how we understand our perception.

If we lean towards physicalism, we might believe that our experiences are the result of specific brain activities. For example, when we see a gorgeous painting, there's a part of our brain lighting up, processing colors, shapes, and emotions. Understanding this can help doctors or scientists find ways to enhance or even repair our perceptions.

On the other hand, if we believe in dualism, our perception isn't just about neurons firing away. It's a deeper interaction between our soul and our senses. This idea could explain phenomena hard to pin down scientifically, like gut feelings or spiritual experiences.

In Essence...

The Mind-Body Puzzle is like a fascinating riddle, one that humanity has been trying to solve for ages. While we might not have all the answers, understanding this debate helps us appreciate the marvel of our existence. Are we sophisticated biological machines, or soulful beings with an ethereal essence? Or perhaps a bit of both?

As we navigate the chapters ahead, we'll dive deeper into the wonders of perception, equipped with the insights from this age-old debate. Our journey of understanding is just getting started!

Chapter 4: Beyond the Five - The Hidden Senses

We all know the main five - sight, hearing, taste, smell and touch. But did you know your body comes equipped with other senses too? These hidden gems often escape the spotlight, yet they play a vital role in your perception.

Let's shed some light on these unsung sensory heroes!

Sensing Within - Interoception and Proprioception

Interoception is your sixth sense - your internal radar, tuning into signals within your body. The gnawing of hunger, the flutter of your heartbeat, even your sense of well-being. Meanwhile, proprioception is your body's spatial positioning system. Ever wonder how touching your nose while closing your eyes is possible? Proprioception is to thank for that!

These overlooked senses provide an inner compass that profoundly impacts how you experience the outer world. Could you truly perceive reality without knowing your own place within it?

Balancing the Elements - Equilibrioception

Equilibrioception, another stealthy sense, keeps you grounded by monitoring balance. Working with your eyes and inner ear, it allows you to walk, run, jump and move without falling on your face!

So the next time you're able to ride a bike or stand on one foot without toppling over, take a moment to appreciate equilibrioception quietly working its magic.

Our hidden senses prove perception is never one dimensional. By tuning into our internal worlds, they allow us to fully inhabit the external one. The next time you feel a gut instinct or move without thinking, remember - not all perception happens through the well-known five.

Ready to dig deeper into these sensory secrets? Let's turn the page!

Chapter 5: Synesthesia - Painting with All the Colors of Our Senses

Picture this: Every time you hear a piano note, you see a vivid burst of color. Or perhaps, every letter you read has its unique taste. Sounds like a whimsical fairy tale, right? But for some people, this blending of senses is their daily reality. This phenomenon is called synesthesia.

A Symphony of Colors and Flavors

At its heart, synesthesia is like a spontaneous art project where the senses mix and mingle in unexpected ways. While most of us experience our senses separately – we hear sounds, see sights, taste flavors – those with synesthesia might "see" sounds or "taste" words.

Imagine opening a box of crayons and finding out that each crayon not just colors but also sings a tune or smells like a specific scent. That's a tiny glimpse into the world of synesthesia.

Walking in Their Shoes: Personal Tales of Synesthesia

Lucy's Rainbow of Sounds: For Lucy, every day is a colorful concert. Whenever she hears music, her world lights up in hues of blues, reds, and golds. A flute might paint delicate lavender strokes, while a drum brings splashes of fiery red.

Ethan's Tasty Alphabet: Ethan has a unique relationship with words. Each letter, for him, has a distinct flavor. The letter 'A' might taste like fresh apple, while 'S' is always a salty sensation. Reading a book is not just a literary feast but also a culinary journey for him.

But, Why? Exploring the 'Why' Through Studies

While synesthesia might sound like magic, scientists have been diving deep to understand it. It's believed that in synesthetes (people with synesthesia), certain areas of the brain, responsible for different senses, are more interconnected than usual. It's like having roads in your brain that connect neighboring towns (senses) more closely.

For example, a study with brain scans showed that when synesthetes "saw" colors while hearing sounds, both their visual and auditory brain regions lit up in harmony. In contrast, for most of us, only the auditory part would light up.

A Beautiful Blend

Synesthesia isn't a disorder or a problem; it's a different, enchanting way of perceiving the world. It reminds us that perception is deeply personal and varied. What might be a mere sound to one can be a vivid canvas of colors to another.

As we journey through the mysteries of perception, synesthesia stands out as a testament to the endless possibilities of how we can experience the world. It's a splash of unexpected color, a twist in the tale, and a reminder of the wonders our senses hold.

Ready for more surprises? Let's continue our adventure and see what other marvels await us!

Chapter 6: Sensory Augmentation and Enhancement

We all want superpowers, don't we? Who wouldn't want bionic senses to see farther, hear more clearly, and experience the world in extraordinary ways? New technologies are making this dream closer to reality than ever.

But with great sensory power comes great responsibility. Let's explore these perception-boosting innovations through an ethical lens.

Enhanced Senses

Sensory augmentation tools like infrared goggles or hearing aids give people superhuman abilities. But some high-tech gadgets raise tricky questions. What if X-ray vision becomes possible? Should we filter what people perceive?

Biohacking - modifying our natural senses through surgery or implants - is already happening too. If you could have your sight or hearing digitally enhanced, would you? At what point could we stop being human and become more machine than biology?

Drawing the Ethical Lines

While sensory aids can restore lost perception or help people in need, recreationally enhancing our senses for fun enters ethically murky waters. Shortcuts to stimulation without skill or effort could make us lose touch with meaningful human experiences.

As we'll see, perception is imperfect by nature. Before chasing technological enhancements, let's reexamine the beauty already within our biological senses.

Superhuman senses offer thrilling possibilities, but may come at a cost if misused. As we stand on this augmented reality precipice, we must think carefully about how to ethically transcend the limits of human perception.

Let's reflect on this more as we turn the page!

Chapter 7: Hallucinations and Illusions - When Our Senses Play Tricks

Imagine you're strolling through a desert, and suddenly, you spot an oasis with lush palm trees and glistening water. Your heart jumps in joy, but as you get closer, it vanishes! It was a mirage. Or think of that viral image of the dress some people swore was blue and black, while others were certain it was white and gold. Why do we sometimes see or hear things that aren't there, or perceive them differently from others?

Welcome to the intriguing world of hallucinations and illusions!

A Glimpse into Illusions

An illusion is like a magician's trick, a little nudge that makes us believe something is there when it isn't. It plays on the usual ways we process information, giving our senses a playful twist. Common examples include:

Mirrors and Light: Think of that oasis mirage. When light rays bend due to the hot and cold air in the desert, it makes us think there's water on the ground.

Optical Puzzles: Ever stared at a spiral drawing and felt it moving? Or seen images where the lines seem crooked but are straight? These optical illusions play with our eyes, making static things appear dynamic or straight lines seem wavy.

Hallucinations: Stories from the Mind

While illusions play with our external senses, hallucinations come from within. They're like dreams while we're awake. A person experiencing a hallucination might hear, see, or even feel something that isn't present.

Examples include:

Whispers in Silence: Some people might hear voices when no one is speaking.

Phantom Sensations: Amputees might sometimes feel pain, itchiness, or sensations in a limb that's no longer there.

Shifting Shadows: In dim light or during high stress, someone might see figures or shapes that aren't real.

What Can These Tricks Tell Us?

Hallucinations and illusions are not mere quirks. They reveal the complex machinery of our perception. Here's how:

Brain's Predictive Power: Our brain is always trying to predict and make sense of the world. Sometimes, in its eagerness, it might fill in the gaps with hallucinations or get fooled by illusions.

Adaptability: Our senses adapt to repeated stimuli. For instance, if you stare at a waterfall and then look at the rocks beside it, they might seem to be moving upwards. This 'motion aftereffect' shows how our visual system adapts and resets.

Emotions and Expectations: Our feelings or what we expect to see can shape our perceptions. If you're scared in a dark room, you might 'see' menacing figures which are just coats hanging on a peg.

While it might be unnerving to think our senses can deceive us, these phenomena remind us of the intricate dance between our external world and our internal processing systems. They highlight that perception is not just a passive reception of information, but an active, creative, and sometimes flawed interpretation of it.

So the next time you're fooled by a playful illusion or a trick of the mind, take a moment to marvel at the wondrous, intricate machinery of perception. It's a reminder that there's always more than meets the eye, or ear, or hand.

Join us in the next chapter as we dive deeper into the rabbit hole of our senses and perceptions!

Chapter 8: Sensory Deprivation - Void of Perception

Picture yourself adrift in a lightless, soundless sea of oblivion, cut off from all sensory input. No smells, no touches, nothing for your perception to grab onto. You are left alone with your thoughts in the most absolute way.

This eerie void is the realm of sensory deprivation. Let's dive into the fascinating effects it has on the mind.

Unmooring the Mind

Without sensory stimuli, people report losing their sense of time and even self. Hallucinations emerge from the darkness of prolonged isolation.

Studies confirm sensory deprivation disrupts cognition. But could this void also offer clarity? Brief sensory fasting may help us reset overloaded minds in our hyper-stimulating world.

Lessons from the Void

The deprivation void teaches us perception's true purpose - bridging the gap between inner mind and outer reality. When that bridge disappears, our very identities seem to hang in the balance.

This mysterious darkness reminds us to cherish the technicolor, scents, and sounds of everyday perception. For without them, where are we?

Sensory deprivation, though unsettling, reveals just how essential perception is in weaving the vibrant tapestry of our reality. Silence this jarring invites us to rediscover that tapestry's beauty with fresh eyes.

Shall we resurface from the void and dive back into perception's light? Let's turn the page!

Chapter 9: Virtual and Augmented Realities - Stepping into Tomorrow's World Today

Have you ever worn those cool glasses or headsets, finding yourself in a bustling alien marketplace or seeing digital dinosaurs roam your backyard? If yes, then you've touched the boundaries of virtual and augmented realities (VR & AR). It's like diving into a dream while you're awake, or sprinkling a dash of magic onto the real world. But how is this shaping our perception, and where is it taking us?

The Magic Behind the Screen

Before we leap ahead, let's grasp the basics:

Virtual Reality (VR): It immerses you entirely in a different world. When you put on those VR goggles, you can find yourself swimming with dolphins, skydiving, or even walking on Mars.

Augmented Reality (AR): This doesn't take you to a different world. Instead, it adds digital elements to your current environment. Remember the Pokemon Go craze? That's AR, where little creatures appeared in your local park or cafe through your phone's screen.

Technology's Role in Redefining Perception

Extended Reality: Both VR and AR are pushing the boundaries of what we call reality. They're making us question what's real and what's digital. For instance, surgeons now train using VR, practicing complex procedures in a virtual operating theater before they tackle the real thing.

Empathy Machines: Ever heard the saying, "Walk a mile in someone's shoes?" VR can make this metaphorical phrase a reality. By immersing users in the experiences of others, it allows them to feel what it's like to be in a war zone, face discrimination, or even be another species!

Enriched Interactions: AR is turning our everyday world into an interactive canvas. Imagine wearing glasses that display reviews above a cafe as you walk by or seeing digital art floating around in a public park.

Navigating the Ethical Labyrinth

As with all great powers, there are great responsibilities. And the realm of VR and AR is no exception.

Reality Distortion: When the virtual feels too real, it might blur the lines between reality and fiction. Can it lead to confusion, or even an addiction to an alternative world?

Privacy Concerns: With AR devices scanning our environment constantly, what happens to the data? There's potential for invasive ads or even surveillance.

Emotional Manipulation: If VR can make us feel intense emotions, could it be misused? Imagine virtual scenarios created just to manipulate feelings or opinions.

The Future: Beyond the Horizon

The journey of VR and AR is just starting:

Tactile Feedback: In the future, you won't just see or hear the virtual world. You might feel the rain on your skin or the cat's fur under your fingers.

Integrated Realities: Imagine a world where your morning mirror gives you news updates, or your window turns into a movie screen at night.

Collective Experiences: Concerts, classes, or even vacations might be attended in shared virtual spaces, connecting people from all over the globe.

Virtual and Augmented Realities are like the telescopes of the 21st century, letting us peer into worlds once deemed impossible. While they're shaping our perceptions in mind-bending ways, they also bring along a baggage of responsibilities.

But one thing's certain: they're expanding the canvas of our experiences, proving that reality, as we know it, is just the beginning. Ready for the next leap? Let's keep exploring, for the universe of perception is vast and wondrous. Onward to the next frontier!

Chapter 10: Towards a More Comprehensive Understanding

Throughout our journey, we've explored perception from different angles - through the senses, the brain, even altered states of consciousness. But a bigger picture is coming into focus.

Advances across fields are converging to unravel perception's remaining mysteries. Let's gaze ahead at what these breakthroughs might reveal.

**Perception Under the Microscope **

Like brain imaging unlocking neural fireworks behind our senses, new technologies peer deeply into perception's inner workings. Philosophers dissect the mind-body problem. Psychologists study quirks like synesthesia.

Each discipline offers another glimpse into the complex kaleidoscope that is perception. Together, a unified understanding awaits.

Where Are We Headed?

These pieces could form a new framework for perceiving our existence. One where subjective experiences coexist with objective measurements in explaining reality.

Will we develop new languages for conveying our sensorium? Perhaps even directly share perceptual moments? The possibilities are as boundless as perception itself!

The next horizon of human progress may be conceptual - mastering perception is the key. With so much still unsolved, our journey promises to be filled with insight and wonder.

Shall we go forth, our view of reality maturing with every step? Onward and upward!

Conclusion: Transcending Perception - Doors to New Dimensions

As we reach the end of this enlightening journey, let's take a moment to breathe and marvel at the intricate tapestry of perception. It's like discovering an art piece where each brushstroke, color, and texture contributes to the overall masterpiece. But what have we truly unearthed, and where do these revelations lead us?

Journey Recap: Revelations and Realizations

The Core of Perception: Our senses, as we've learned, are the gateways to how we perceive the world. They are our primary tools in experiencing the vivid, bustling universe around us.

Mind Games: From the debates of dualism vs. physicalism to the puzzles our own brain can play on us (like hallucinations), we've learned that our mind is an enigma, ever-evolving and deeply fascinating.

Synesthesia & Sensory Blends: We discovered that perception can be fluid, with some of us experiencing blended senses, painting the world in more colors and sounds than we could imagine.

Tech's Hand in Reality: With VR & AR, we realized that our perception isn't limited to what nature offers. We can stretch it, augment it, and immerse ourselves in entirely new universes.

The Future: A Canvas Awaiting Paint

Understanding perception is more than a mere intellectual exercise. It's a compass pointing us towards a future where:

Enhanced Empathy: Understanding perception can lead to deeper connections. If we can truly grasp how others perceive the world, empathy becomes a more authentic experience.

Breakthrough Innovations: Knowledge about how we perceive paves the way for tech innovations, be it in entertainment, medicine, or education. Imagine therapies built around personal perception profiles or learning modules tailored to how one best perceives information.

Unlocking Human Potential: Grasping our perception might just be the key to unlocking potentials we never knew we had. Could we develop a sixth sense? Can we train our minds to perceive beyond the conventional?

Final Musings: The Universe Within

In diving deep into perception, we've not just explored the external world but have journeyed inward, into the universe that exists within each of us. It's a reminder that each person's reality is unique, molded by the distinctive way they perceive.

And as we stand on this precipice of understanding, we can't help but wonder: If perception shapes reality, by understanding and perhaps even altering our perception, could we not shape our reality?

The doors to countless dimensions beckon, with perception being the key. And as we continue our quest in understanding, we must remember: The only limits are those we perceive.

Here's to transcending boundaries, unlocking new dimensions, and embracing the endless possibilities of perception. The journey has just begun!

About Freudian Trips

Welcome to Freudian Trips, your dedicated platform for diving deep into the world of psychology. We are more than just a YouTube channel or a book publisher. We are a beacon of enlightenment, making complex psychological concepts accessible and engaging for all.

Our YouTube channel is a rich repository of psychology made simple. We take the profound and often complex ideas from the world of psychology and break them down into digestible, easy-to-understand content. From the foundational theories of Freud to the cognitive insights of Piaget, we cover a broad spectrum of psychological schools and thoughts, making psychology accessible to everyone, regardless of their background or prior knowledge.

As a book publisher, we take the same approach, transforming intricate psychological theories into comprehensible narratives. Our books are not just collections of words, but vessels of wisdom that make psychology approachable and relatable. We believe that psychology should not be confined to academic circles, but should be available to all who seek to understand the human mind and behavior.

At Freudian Trips, we believe in the power of curiosity and the pursuit of knowledge. We are here to stoke the fires of your curiosity, to guide you on your intellectual journey, and to help you navigate the fascinating world of psychology.

If you are someone who is not afraid to question, to explore, and to learn, then you are in the right place. Join us on this journey of exploration, as we make psychology easy to understand, one concept at a time.

Be sure to visit our Youtube channel at: www.freudiantrips.com/youtube

You can also visit us on the web at www.freudiantrips.com

Welcome to The Freudian Trip community. Stay curious. Stay enlightened.